Holistic Wisdom

I0081910

Increase your
Strength, Health, Wealth and Love

by

Paul George Smith Jr.
and Community

ISBN-13: 978-0692721285

Dedication

This simple book is dedicated to you.

Table of Contents

Foreword

Vincent Van Gogh, the infamous Dutch impressionist painter once said, *"Great things are done by a series of small things brought together."* Paul George Smith Jr. certainly exemplifies this truism in his creative anthology – bringing to the world the wisdom he and his friends offer from a place of reflection and grace. A man of actually few words, yet a lot of mindful action, Paul has amassed many, many friends throughout the world in his travels and studies. Striving for the ego-less characteristics of the mentors and sages from which he gained his holistic wisdom, it is no surprise to me that Paul's book would highlight the words and prose of those he cares deeply about.

As the founder of one of the largest private colleges for holistic wellness education in America, I was engrossed in rapt delight as I read the words of those Paul calls his friends, and I call students, graduates, and instructors. The mission of the college is to inspire individuals to discover their gifts. Paul's unique gifts are collaborating and community building. Whether it is serving in the Peace Corp, hiking the mountains of Nepal, living through a near-death experience to tell about it, or coming to the base of Mt. Everest in complete humility and gratitude, Paul knows his life mission is to teach and create teams of healers. While it might sound trite to refer to Paul as a 'pied piper', it is most accurate to say he is a 'modern shaman', with the ability to 'hold space' for those with pipe-dreams. Paul is the earth to those around him who live in the ethers and dance over the fires of life. Paul has wisdom beyond his years, exhibiting uncanny, intuitive abilities and a committed interest in creating an impact on the world, while also creating financial abundance for himself and his many friends.

Paul clearly states as the intention for this this 'divinely inspired' book, is to bring together a community of wonderful humans, healers, and heroes who have chosen to share their insights. You are invited to benefit from this collection of *'wholistic wisdom'* – wise thoughts, talking points, and 'realized truths' from a whole commuUNITY dedicated to UNITY.

"Alone we can do so little; together we can do so much," said Helen Keller. Paul George Smith, Jr., and Friends offer much. It has been said that when two or more are gathered, the angels sing ~ Listen for the sound of angels as your read.

Blessings,

KC Miller
Founder of Southwest Institute of Healing Arts
#Seeker and #Teacher

Acknowledgments

Thank you to my family
for your amazing love and support

Thank you to my friends
for sharing your friendship

Thank you to my teachers
for the guidance

Thank you to my professional colleagues
for sharing your wisdom and skill

Thank you to everyone
who contributed content to this project

Thank you in advance to everyone
whom I have yet to meet

You all teach me so much

You're all my gurus

Eternal gratitude

Introduction

"I am not a genius, I am just curious. I ask many questions. and when the answer is simple, then God is answering."
- Albert Einstein

"Modern civilization is complicated and artificial. Simple folk live in a world of love and peace."
- Sivananda Saraswati

"If you can't explain it simply, you don't understand it well enough."
- Albert Einstein

This book is unique since it is
simple
to the point
and practical

I could write millions of words -
though for now,
just a few will be enough

Sometimes, less is more
in writing

and in life

The perspectives included are unique
some are old
some are new
some are famous
some are unheard of

Wisdom is wisdom
Regardless of who shares it

The prose and structure throughout the book
is intentionally unique
and imperfect

I invite you to read
with adaptability

I invite you to experiment
with doing the same in life

The entire text is "centered"
in the middle of the pages

I hope this helps invoke a sense
of being "centered"
and "in alignment"
with yourself

I invite you to question everything

Test it for yourself

Experiment

The information is adaptable

Personalize it for yourself

Don't take my word for it
Take only your own word

These are only my opinions
and only the opinions of others

See for yourself
and have fun!

"Do not believe in anything simply because you have heard it. Do not believe in anything simply because it is spoken and rumored by many. Do not believe in anything simply because it is found written in your religious books. Do not believe in anything merely on the authority of your teachers and elders. Do not believe in traditions because they have been handed down for many generations. But after observation and analysis, when you find that anything agrees

with reason and is conducive to the good and benefit of one and all, then accept it and live up to it."
- Buddha

Intentions for this book:

1. Bring together a community of wonderful humans and share their insights and inspirations
2. Share quotes from famous experts and change-makers
3. Answer questions from others
4. Share what I've learned and what seems to work for me - and what may work for you
5. Invite you to experiment with thoughts and techniques
6. Open connection and communication for further questions, support and collaboration

---

I hope for you the greatest successes

You're welcome to contact me with your questions and ideas

Best wishes and unconditional love to you!

Paul George Smith Jr.

Long Beach, California
June, 2016

Part I

Community Wisdom

The following are quotes from
my amazing family, friends and colleagues

I sent out open invitations on social media
for anyone to contribute
and am so grateful for the responses

I decided to use this book as an opportunity
to help publish the wisdom of others
instead of just my own

We are stronger together
Healthier together
Wiser together

Thank you all for helping heal the world
with your simple and significant actions
your inspirational words
and your love
every day

"Be actively in love with yourself.

This is the best way to protect your energy.
Love yourself unconditionally,
so that you may truly love another.

There is nothing more empowering than being in love,
with You, and sharing that love with others.

As his Holiness, the Dalai Lama XIV said,
'As you breathe in, cherish Yourself.
As you breathe out, cherish all Beings.'

This my daily mantra.
This is how I breathe.
Love."

- Shung Pak

"Honor yourself and you will honor others.

Surround yourself with those who honor you
and love and peace will be with you forever."

- Lorrie King

"So much pressure on
Was anyone right or wrong
Dark illuminate

Recovery time
Beautiful scars show you lived
You can fly away

So calm so peaceful
Want that to happen, allow
All you desire

The trees whisper it
Winding roads spell it all out
Inherent beauty"

- Aubreyana Bre

"Love Is The Way To Be
Way To Free From Mind Controlling Things
Be Your Self
Believe
In All You Desire Deep
Our Hearts & Senses Are So Intense
Precious
I Must Confess This
I Am Feeling & Projecting
Infinite Affection"

- Kato Tesla

"How do you get stuck if you are dreaming everyday?"

- Rebecca Barbanell
Nesting Grounds

"I see you…love made manifest
in the fabric of existence.
Sacred geometry,
vibrations of sound,
ecstatic glances,
my next breath,
weaving this life in perfect harmony.
I trust your will.
I believe you
when you show me my own strength
by handing me this beautiful life
and saying
"Rejoice in my play,
leave nothing in your heart.
Share all of me.
This is who you are.
Surrender to truth,
And know all is well.

Excruciatingly beautiful.
Living with this reality day in and day out.
Tears shed have lost definition.
The lesson of the pain is equal to the reality of joy.
One coin tossed forever in the air
spinning its knowledge.
This moment
contains
all of life.

There is no seeking required.
Love shines brightly.
Right here.

Right now.

I am sitting here thinking about love
and how to put into words what I am feeling
Now a bird just came and sang his song outside my window
It is 11 pm, all is still and dark
this bird...
this moment...
This is Love"

- Lavina Singh

"Natural Freedom

Take a stroll with me,
And I'll help u see,
The world In a new light.
The secret treasures,
Intimate bonds,
Hid in plain sight.
Warp your mind,
To lose all thought,
And drip away,
At one alone.
The robotic dance,
And endless cage,
Of never deciding on your own.
This is freedom,
The crucial ebb,
In the wave of life's recede.
In this moment,
Basic senses,
Be all u ever need.
The sense of touch,
In a whimsical manner,
Tracing the red rose.
The petals,
Velvet tickle tips,
Gently grazed across your nose.
The smell,
A sweet enchanting scent,
That travels to your core.
And then in sight,
You gaze upon,
Ruby red,
And crave more.

Smell of floral high society,
You cant help but taste maroon. Intoxicated by the ambiance,
The high left way too soon.
A bit a dazed and still elated,
You ponder an ambitious cue.
If a single rose,
Can lend such magic,
Imagine what the rest of nature can do. Thus why,
It is our purpose,
To respect Mother earth,
Because, in the grand scheme of things, it is from she,
That we were birthed."

- Latoya Fields Wagoner

"What is the path to perfection? Must we achieve it?

_____

The path to perfection is discovery of your
inner beauty and purpose in life.

You don't have to be perfect to everybody
you just have to be perfect to somebody.
Remember that somebody can be you!

Love yourself first,
for true perfection comes
from the love we radiate
onto ourselves."

- Stephanie Giermek

"You have lived such an amazing, adventurous life so far,
and have plans already for your next adventure.
How do you bring that into your everyday life?

I live each day like an adventure.
I wake up each day and do not get out of bed
until I can smile a genuine smile.
A smile for what I experienced the day before.
A smile of gratitude for the opportunities today
and a smile of wonderment for what today will bring."

- Viki Kibodeaux

"My life has been a Wild Ride, and I would not change a thing!
If I did, I wouldn't BE the culmination of the spiritual gifts
which I have received. I am so grateful for the 'Good & Not So
Good' chapters of my Life, as they have brought me here to a
'deeper spiritual truth', for my purpose here on Earth, to BE a
shining example of Love, Joy, Peace, Happiness, & Compassion
& more! Now, in my 40's, I Am finally living MY BLISS
and my authentic Truth!

I no longer bathe in Fear or Guilt, and I now know that, we are
never alone, and are fully supported, by our higher power (God,
Universe, Spirit, Jesus, Angels, Buddha, or whatever you choose to
call your I AM!) Those who carry Spirit in their hearts
are one with Spirit.

~I AM Love!
~I AM Joy!
~I AM Peace!
~I AM Faith!
~I AM Powerful!
~I Am Grace, Courage & Wisdom!
~I AM all things....as WE are Connected as part of One
Community!"

- Ronna Faith Ambrosino

"Some things I've learned by reaching for truth within and
throughout my bodies to find self love
that was once lost but now is found.

All things are possible.
Love is more than most perceive.
Love is in all things.

Experience is key to learning the value of life.

With love in our hearts we can do anything
we are given the opportunity to receive.

When we are well, we are balanced,
we are happy, we are healthy.

When we are at dis-ease, we are imbalanced,
we are sad or mad, we are sick.

Better to make a change than not transform at all,
because time and space are not constant.

We make our own decisions,
our own choice,
to be who we are.

Not a single person is exactly the same
with how they manifest their outward appearances.

We are all the same on the inside.

Meditation allows for guidance from the internal connection within yourself. By taking a journey within, you are taking the chance that you might see all of you, your physical body, your emotions, your mental abilities, your gifts and connections with all that is.

That connection established with the energy that surrounds me helps me understand self love in way that can't be described with words; it is a feeling. The connection I've felt with the earth and the universe, supporting me and protecting me, my ancestors guiding me through my own body, healing generations before me through my transformation of DNA. It's through self love that we find ourselves and everything connected to help create an earth that heals itself.

With love, awareness and intention
we can heal all things."

- Jessie Cleveland

"We can begin at the very beginning, when all there was was Spirit. So many describe Source rightly as WHOLENESS, and they say God is ONE. But what is wholeness and what is oneness, and is there any difference at all?

Oneness is described as being WHOLE or in a state of WHOLENESS even though the subject in question is made up of TWO or MORE parts.

WHOLENESS then is considered a concept where one contains all potentials for movement, thought, sound, creation, etc…

God is often times represented in the sacred geometry as a simple circle or sphere. But this seems incomplete, especially when feminine energy is related to curved lines where straight lines are considered masculine. Isn't God both masculine and feminine?

Consider though, every circle has a diameter. And if you take a sphere and at it's core, extend straight lines through from inner surface to inner surface, you have the geometry for both masculine energy.

I could not understand though how a line could be ONENESS if it was supposed to be the representation of 2 separate parts. Then I took the line, which is the number 1, and rotated it in my mind to where I was looking at it from the top down and saw ONE FIXED POINT! Then it hit me. If I were to rotate the line 180* then the 2nd POINT would be visible. There for a number one is an accurate model of the nature of the ONENESS of SPIRIT (masculine) and a circle is the representation of the WHOLENESS of LOVE/SOURCE (feminine).

Ancient mathematicians came up with the symbol for Phi which is a circle with a line drawn straight through the center.

Looks like the partial representation of a taurus doesn't it? The diagram fits perfectly to the electromagnetic flow from the human heart which is also seen in the electromagnetic gravitational flow of the earth from pole to pole.

Therefore, we are living energy, extensions from the Source if you will, replications of the Creative Force that made/makes us, connected and yet individual like petals of a flower."

- Nicole M Mitchell

"Since ancient times on our planet, we have learned numerous health and wellness practices. I have found that many of the effective health and wellness practices are often very simple. For instance, taking a moment in a quiet serene setting (preferably in nature) to close your eyes, go within and take some deep breaths. This simple practice can offer many benefits.

Here are 5 simple awarenesses
to living a healthy and prosperous life:

The food we eat: In this day and age its almost more important knowing what to avoid and not put into your body. There are so many toxic packaged foods and drinks that exist today, that its important to read labels and be aware of ingredients. Buying organic, non-GMO, unpackaged foods as much as possible is strongly recommended. From my experience, shopping at local farmers markets and growing your own food are the most sustainable and healthy options.

The water we drink: Water is the source of all life on our planet. Our planet and the human body are both made up of around 70% water. Its important to drink plenty of water. Both city tap water and bottled water are found to contain chemicals that are toxic to our health. I've found that natural spring water and water ran through some type of filtration system are the most sustainable and healthy options.

The air we breathe: Its often hard for us to control the quality of the air that were breathing. Especially for those of us living in big cities. Going into nature for doses of fresh, non-polluted air is a great balance from the city air we often breathe each day.

The exercise we get: We have the ability to walk, run, dance, and move in amazing ways with our bodies. Today, many people are out of tune with their bodies and have forgotten the importance of movement and exercise. Having some form of movement or exercise routine is an important part of this human experience and will do wonders for your health and wellness.

The thoughts we think: Out of all 5 of these awarenesses, I consider the thoughts that we think to be the most important aspect to fulfilling optimal health and wellness. Its important to remember that we are not our thoughts. Many people who suffer from depression and other health problems can gain so much from thinking more positive, uplifting thoughts. As you may have already discovered, our thoughts can change our realities.
I am very honored for this opportunity to share my truth with such an amazing community supporting this book. Wishing everyone a joyous and prosperous journey of life."

- Ryan Prosper Sanchez

"I exercise to get stronger, stay active and keep my body moving. I exercise to de-stress. Whenever feeling stressed out I have to find a way to relieve stress and all the pent-up energy inside me. I feel like exercising helps me focus on one thing rather than multiple things at once. I also release all of that stress. Whenever I exercise I like to go outside because I think getting some fresh air and sunlight is helpful. I feel like I connect with nature."

- Alyssa Tejeda

"Baggy eyes? That's probably swollen kidneys.

No. It's not that you are aging and now you have bags under your eyes. It's vice versa – you eat toxic crap, chew on toxic relationships and that is why you are aging.

One look at your face can tell me more about you than all the words you say. I can tell you what you eat for breakfast, lunch, and dinner. I can tell you how you sleep or not.
I can tell you how your love life is…

And no amount of make-up, no amount Dolce Gabbana or Luis Vuitton is gonna fill the void within you. The truth is you crave and you eat to cheer yourself up. And it's all in your face.

You crave love. You walk around begging for love. How long do you wanna live like that? Do you really believe anything from outside can fill you in? Do you believe this guy or that guy will finally prove you worthy of love? Or that next thing you wanna buy? Or your to-do-list will prove you lovable?

You fill that void with the food you stuff into you mouth. And – it's not so good, not so vibrant for you…

Surprised you lack energy? Age? Gain? Lose? Surprised you and your loved ones develop cancer, diabetes, autoimmune disorder, Hashimoto?

It's all in your face. The ancient art of facial diagnosis. You will be afraid to sit in the tube and watch people. You will be frightened with what you see at the airports or at the beach.
Inflammation. Constipation. Addiction.

It's all in your face.
Your face never lies.
Detox, Babe. Time to Detox."

- Evita Ramparte
Author of Badass Detox and other works

"Keep Reinventing Yourself

'You're never too old to set another goal or dream a new dream.'
~C. S. Lewis

Change is the only constant thing and change means reinvention.
A change in job, a change in relationship,
moving to a different abode or losing a loved one -
each and every major shift in life demands reinvention.
We have one of the two options: either we reinvent ourselves,
take control of who we will become or risk
never reaching our full potential,
living our dream or even having a life.

In today's unstable, fragile economic society there is always
a fear masking the environment.
The fear of going to work one day
and not having a job the next day.
The fear of the unknown!!!

Hence, it is important to continue learning and continue
reinventing ourselves not by force but by choice.
I believe it's important to choose reinvention
even before the tragedy strikes.
Instead of waiting in vain for the future to find us,
it would be better if we take control of our future and forge
ourselves on a new path
deliberately and with foresight.

'Destiny is not a matter of chance. It is a matter of choice. It is not to be waited for, it is a thing to be achieved'
~ William Jennings Bryan

But before we jump into reinventing ourself, we need to slow down, reflect, and spend some time writing down our thoughts. We spend too much time and energy focusing on today's immediate concerns or chasing the wrong dream. Without a clear assessment of our past, present and future situation and an effective approach to pursuing our goals, we can end up sick, broke or lonely- a future we would never want. We need to ask ourselves the reason for our reinvention and then come up with a list of all the big and small changes needed to make reinvention happen. Creating a gameplay and coming up with a timeline to make those changes will ensure that we stay on track during this journey.

The path to reinvention could be a roller coaster ride. If we want to get closer to reinventing ourself, then we need to stay positive and motivated throughout this journey. Focusing on the solutions rather than the problems, clearing the negativity from life, surrounding ourselves with like minded people who support our reinvention, finding ways to reduce unwanted stress and staying mentally strong would ensure we win the battle towards our reinvention.

Looking at the big picture, projecting ourselves deep into the future and asking ourselves, " What is it that we really want to do and will regret not having done?" and then working backwards to achieve that goal will give us a roadmap to plan our life and a reason to live.

Remember that the path to reinvention is an opportunity of our time to discard what we think we know and instead learn what we need to learn. Every single day. Keep reinventing yourself!

About the Author:

Parul Agrawal is an International Bestselling Author, Huffington Post Blogger, Bestselling Book Publisher & Coach, the host of a soon-to-be launched Mama Podcast and Publishing Director of Transformational CEO LLC. She is one of India's leading online female entrepreneur with a mission to educate families and professionals alike about simple but extremely effective ways to live healthier, happier and successful lives.

Her friends say that she has the technical brain of an engineer, the (w)holistic mindset of a naturopathic/fitness health coach and the infinite patience of a mom. It is her pleasure to use these varied and diverse skills to help individuals achieve optimal physical, spiritual, emotional and financial well-being.

You can find more about her at www.parulagrawal.com and she is available on Facebook, LinkedIn, Twitter by Author Parul.

Other Websites:

www.prenatalnourish.com
www.amazonmidwife.com
www.transformationalceo.com"

- Parul Agrawal

"So much rising with mindfulness in the past several weeks,
at any given moment an opportunity to be reminded and
awaken to my true calling.
Now more apparent than ever the work that is to be done.

As we were speaking of earlier; so often in this journey we start
down a path with full awareness and intention; embracing the
possibility of life change. As we continue; the human aspects of
self (the little me) comes into play. At a time of abundance and
openness and relationship - connection, we may second guess our
decisions as possibly wrong, selfish, irresponsible. "Why would I
choose to leave all that is being presented to me; to go and
abandon what is... for the unknown, the unpredictable"?

The truth may actually be that continuing to move forward,
embracing the jagged edginess to the unknown may be what we
need in order to continue to break away the ego, the sense of self,
who I am (again the little me), the letting go of layers...healing in
deep profound ways- ancestrally- past lives. What is needed to
polish the rough edges, polish the mirror, allow the true self- who
we truly are- to shine forth. We don't get there through
preconceived notions of who we are; we get there through the
roughness, the jagged edges, the uncomfortable moments that force
us to shed our skin and be born again. The complete surrender,
surrender in ways we never knew possible,
in order to trust that we are supported, that we are whole.
That we are perfect in all our imperfection.
That the one and only thing we are and ever were is love.

In the last week or so, I have witnessed mindfulness through
breath, devastation at the loss of a loved one.. several times.. I've
looked on as displays of innocence and pure joy spread across a

beautiful young face. I've wept tears of gratitude as my hands dug in the earth, planting seeds of intentions. I've fallen to my knees in both overwhelming abundance and pain. Replayed memories of a chapter about to close, This is the life we are presented and we make a choice to watch as an observer or to partake as an active participant. To embrace or to deny. To question or surrender. All of this- this Maya- illusion- is but a play; we are mere actors. And even as we realize that we are all in this together, we are one, we are connected - we choose. We choose to be love or to close and bury ourselves in preconceived thoughts of right and wrong. There are no accidents, all is as it should be. Only this moment, this breath is guaranteed. Forgive, Surrender, Love.

It may start with mindfulness of breath. Just the simple act of breathing; how it feels, how it moves. Then awareness of thought; compassion that we are likely to be in thought often and instead of trying to manipulate it, or ban it- give it some love. Acknowledge it and then gently come back to the breath. Next awareness of body; how does the body feel? Tangible mass, heart pumping, blood circulating, breath moving. Sensations, emotions. The constant flow of energy and vibration is this ever changing this structure. It starts with this. When we can be mindful of these elements of being, we are training ourselves to be in the ebb and flow. the ups and downs, the peaks and valley's. We are embracing to meet our emotional selves with more clarity and equanimity. In this mindful state we are able to be more receptive, more open to experience life, even when it is intense.Fear and feelings of being overwhelmed, separateness,not enough- not whole start to dissipate. Intensity may often lead to the biggest growth periods in our human journey. Mindfulness changes what rises in our experience. We are able to meet life with more kindness, love, compassion. Less anger, worry. We can be mindful of judgements whether our own or someone else's which will then allow us to be open to the exploration of the journey instead of trying to control

or make it stop. Once we can be mindful of self the ego slips away, we recognize that we are all connected and are able to loose the sense of separateness. This- This is the true gift. The ability to be completely present. Aware of our breath, our bodies, our thoughts.. sensations and emotions. What allows us to love and be love.
A miraculous, beautiful gift."

- Lanita Ugstad

"LOVE

We have all been given the gift of being human, of life as we know it. It is meant to be hard, we are meant to have challenges, we are meant to learn. As different as we all are in backgrounds, culture, social standing, etc. we are all the same in our humanness. We all have fears and anxieties. We sometimes lie and cheat. We are prone to be selfish and sometimes victims. We hurt, we feel guilt, we feel shame. We have ego and sometimes judge or blame. We have pride and jealousy. We try to hide our insecurities. We have failures, and make mistakes. We suffer from illness, and physical and emotional pain. We sometimes are victims of abuse or crime. We sometimes commit abuse or crimes. We lose loved ones, we mourn. We hurt in our core, a gnawing pain in our soul.
But................

We have also been given the gift of love. Love transcends all. Love brings out our goodness, our kindness, our compassion. Love helps us to forgive and to heal. Love makes us feel whole, gives us purpose. Love helps us to change for the better. Love gives us faith. Love and faith combined are powerful. Love and faith help us overcome addictions. Love and faith make miracles. We become the best version of ourselves. What helps us to love and have faith? Prayer. Prayer lifts the veil between our humanness and our spirituality. Prayer gives us revelation. The little voice within us becomes more alive. We become more intuitive and have a "knowing". Listen to that still, small voice my friends. This is God. This is the Universe. This is the higher power instructing us, guiding us to our life's purpose.

TURNING SIXTY

Now that I'm fifty-nine it never occurred to me to prepare for turning sixty as if it were a major milestone. My younger cousin visited me recently, and since it had been awhile since we had seen each other we spoke about how old we were getting. He thought turning sixty was going to be a big day for me. Frankly, I hadn't even thought about it. So here I am now pondering for the first time what it will be like to reach my sixth decade. Well I certainly feel wiser. I have grown as a human being. I am more in touch with my spirit, with God, with love, with service. I am comfortable in my skin. I have learned much. I have learned that love is the most important gift in life. How much money we have, how much stuff we've accumulated, or how high up the corporate ladder we've climbed are not really that important in the scheme of life. I have learned about the power of forgiveness and gratitude. I have learned to trust in God, to ride the wave of change, to accept when events occur that may hurt, or seem negative or may knock us down. I have learned that when "bad" things happen, they are not really bad. They are God or the Universe guiding us in a different direction, guiding us towards our purpose. Enlightenment is accepting these events as gifts from God, blessing us and leading us to our higher selves, to goodness, to where we are supposed to be, to LOVE.

I don't fear aging. I look forward to it. I am excited to continue to learn. I want to serve others, and share my wisdom and my lessons. Love is about getting out of ourselves and giving to others. I believe that is everyone's life's purpose. Our journeys may lead us in different directions, but each of our roads on our respective journey eventually merges into oneness, merges into LOVE.

Namaste"

- Maria Moretti

MariaMoretti123@yahoo.com

"When we experience upset, we must take responsibility for the disturbance. Because there is an opportunity to awaken more fully. What we want to recognize is when our school is in session."

"Nothing is either right or wrong, it's the thinking that keeps us there. The more conscious you are, the more responsibility you have to see people where they are, accept them and love them."

These are not my own words, they came from my teachers at USM - Ron and Mary Hulnick, where I'm getting my master's in spiritual psychology. I found them in my notes and they resonate with me.

Take care,

Breanna Kulwin

"Forgiveness

Letting go of grudges and Bitterness

Forgiveness is the quickest way to release you from your inner and outer struggles, issues, conflicts and dis-eases.

Many of us believe that to forgive someone for a wrongdoing is to send him or her a message that what he or she did was ok. The opposite is true and the fact is when you forgive someone else for their acts you actually release yourself from the physical, mental, emotional, spiritual distress and disharmony it causes you. When you hold onto such low vibrational energy it stops you from expressing your true God/divine nature into the world and from that mental stance you will struggle to live a spiritually reliable life.

The act of forgiving others is the highest expression of Gods divine nature and is the only way you can truly become free and to move around the cabin of life in harmony, so to speak. When you make a decision to not forgive another for what they did or said to you, then you become firmly belted and restricted into a very limited space lacking possibilities. Think of how you feel when you are sitting in the middle seat in an airplane. Being belted and strapped down onto any chair only keeps you stuck and anchored to a very limited space. In this metaphor I'm describing a very small space with limited room to move, grow and express yourself fully. This small-constricted, confining space may feel safe and comfy, but lacks the open space for true bigger possibility to manifest.

All of us have had acts, words and wrong doings done to us. And, most of those acts of wrongdoing were perceived as painful by our human ego.

Is it possible that these acts of wrongdoing were powerful learning opportunities? Life is full of wrong doings, misfortune, drama and chaos. The light is not the only teacher. The darkness teaches and shows you what you don't want in your life. These experiences never feel peaceful, but come with a message if you let your spirit guide you. As Marianne Williamson writes, "The ego says, "Once everything falls into place, I'll feel peace." The spirit says, "Find your peace, and then everything will fall into place. "When these types of experiences happen to us we take it very personally and our automatic emergency response system goes into high alert and rings the danger bell. These bells signal a rude intrusion, a breach in contract. They beckon and warn you of a threat and possible betrayal to your physical, mental, emotional and spiritual systems. When we hear the bells of betrayal sound out, most of us run, hide, duck and take cover seeking to avoid or minimize our own personal/spiritual attack – this is normal for most of us and is a part of our human programming. This programming is literally hardwired into us from our DNA and goes way back to our primitive self's. This programming is designed to protect us and sends the message to fight or flight – not to forgive those who have hurt our emotional selves.

The process of rewiring our primitive self is not something we naturally do easily. In fact, it will feel very unnatural and odd until you retrain and rewire your mental-chemical programming. In the beginning most people will resist the idea to forgive someone for an act of wrongdoing and will cling to their pain, agony and misery out of sheer fear of being violated again. I am a firm believer and

teach that healing can only begin to take place after you feel the
pain. I always tell my students, who are feeling an old wound
during class to talk it out it, walk it out, run it out, dance it out, do
something with the feelings, but make sure you feel them. In order
to heal you must feel, and then once we feel, we must deal.
Nothing has a hold on your mind that you cannot release. To break
free you will need to go through a spiritual labor and seek to give
birth to your higher self–a higher self is the part of you who can
rise up and be forgiving. It's just a moment where you decide to let
go of right and wrong, bear down to feel the pain you once
experienced. Then begin to apply love to anything that is perceived
as hurt, pain, betrayal and/or a lack of love–in this moment you
will rise up, transcend the old stuck negative stories and feelings
and move into compassion for the wrong doer.
It is like a 1000 pound weight is lifted off your chest and you can
breath again. Most people do not realize how much pressure was
on them until they let it go and forgive. To forgive is extremely
relieving to our mind, body and *spirit*. To forgive is to love, and to
lovingly forgive is to walk a *Spiritually Reliable* life.

Any thoughts of revenge are like cancer eating you from the inside,
which then manifests into your life as pain, sickness, addiction,
isolation, shame, anger, fear and then turns inward and becomes an
even deeper wound that creates a self-sacrificed life.
I asked him if he would be willing to just speak out everything that
was on his mind. He agreed and the torrent began. As he shared it,
it continued to get larger, bigger and longer. It was like the door to
Pandora's box was opened and what exposed itself was
unbelievable darkness, negativity and hatred. All of this was
stealing and robbing him from having a beautiful life, a life where
he walked daily as his greatest, highest, wisest expression of
himself. Instead it was stealing and robbing his authentic personal
power.

If you are still living in the pain of any experience, you may need to feel it for a while. I know that everyone is on his or her own timeline and God will always honor your time by allowing you to choose. Remember there is no wrong path and even the path of pain, can become, in the end, your greatest and wisest teacher.

While journeying down this path of forgiveness I believe you will be in one of three metaphorical models and may vacillate between the mindsets:

1) **Ostrich:** The Ostrich archetype chooses to hang on to the pain of the experience for their own conscious or unconscious reasons. Burying their head in the sand, denying there is anything wrong. Walking in a fog, not able to see clearly or consciously.

2) **Masochist:** The Masochist archetype enjoys the pain—feeling alive because it appears that something is happening in their life. They may be enthralled by the drama, and choose to hang out in it because it's feeding a need within them to feel something, or rather–this is better than nothing.

3) **Warrior:** The Warrior archetype feels the *need* to feel the pain and to learn the lessons by getting squeezed and pushed through the knothole to learn the higher spiritual message. They recreate themselves by learning from their painful experiences.

Feeling the pain can actually transform your life, because it requires you to push through the knothole and once you exit—your life trajectory is altered. This alteration may have been the exact thing that was needed to place you on the path to your next assignment, your next lesson, and a reset. Without this painful experience you would have never made the shifts that were absolutely vital to get you to where you needed to be. These painful experiences are actually fuel that propels you to jump into the gap and begin to brew new possibilities. When you're living in possibility your living positively. When you're positive your energy, your light begins to rise and all those old painful experiences fall away and you begin to transcend the false illusions that you were wronged and replace it with the knowing that every struggle and challenge has a spiritual lesson. A spiritually reliable person will seek to understand and those who seek find.

When someone who you care about hurts you, you can hold on to your anger, resentment and thoughts of revenge, or embrace forgiveness, seek to transcend and move up, forward and onward.

It is important for you to do the work it requires to make this upward leap. Meaning it may require you to seek outside counsel or coaching which will assist you in feeling and healing the wrong doing. As I have stated previously in order for you to heal, you must feel and when you feel you heal.

Nearly everyone has been hurt by the actions or words of another. Perhaps your mother criticized your parenting skills, your colleague sabotaged a project or your partner had an affair. These wounds can leave you with lasting feelings of anger, bitterness or even vengeance—but if you don't practice forgiveness, you might be the one who pays most dearly. By embracing forgiveness, you can also embrace peace, hope, gratitude and joy. Consider how forgiveness can lead you down the path of physical, emotional and spiritual well-being.

As I was writing this chapter my spiritual listening was activated and I was told very clearly to write this down on a post a note:

"Find medical evidence on how not forgiving effects us physically, mentally, emotionally and spiritually." I remember thinking to myself, "Could there be documented evidence?"
I began the quest to find any medical documentation that could validate my intuitional claims. I stumbled upon a very validating article written by the Mayo Clinic labeling unforgiveness as a physical, mental medical condition.
They share that letting go of grudges and bitterness can make way for compassion, kindness and peace.

Forgiveness can lead to:

1)   Healthier relationships both with others and yourself.
2)   Greater spiritual and psychological well-being.
3)   Less anxiety, stress and hostility.
4)   Lower blood pressure.
5)   Fewer symptoms of depression.
6)   Lowers the risk of alcohol and substance abuse

My invitation for you would be to feel the pain as much as you need to feel it. But, understand the longer you hold on to the pain, agony and misery of any experience you are strapped down, held down by someone else's past acts. This causes your life force to be sucked out of you and you are unable to freely move about as a divine expression of God, as a Spiritually Reliable vessel. Or you can choose to be released from all and any past wrong doings, just by the mere claiming it as so, and by and in the authority of God's loving law. Shall we release this truth now into the law of God as Done? Yes! And, so it is!

Grounding Prayer

Dear God,

I acknowledge that I am always unified with your loving, everlasting energy. I choose to lie in the arms of divine flow, and give up my need to make others wrong. I decide now to let go of all grudges and bitterness of others whom I feel have said and done things to me, which hurt me. I reclaim my authority as a divine expression of God by letting go and forgiving others and myself. When I do forgive I know that only then can I freely move about in the world as a bursting expression of the divine spark that was implanted in me at birth. I let go and forgive easily; I let go and allow God's grace to lift me up and over the resistance now.   I release this prayer into the Law of God's as done. And, so it is.

Author Bio:

Richard Seaman is an award winning teacher, spiritual leader, speaker and writer. He is the founder and director of Seattle Life Coach Training (SLCT), and one of the nation's top spiritual authors. Richard's mission is to Train you to Transform Lives through his classes, books and motivational talks and presentations. Please visit him on the web at www.RichardSeamanOnline.com and www.SLCTSeattle.com and www.SLCTSanDeigo.com to discover more about Richard Seaman. To purchase a full copy of his books you can go to www.Amazon.com and type in Richard Seaman."

"Laughter is the best medicine.

Mostly because it makes it easiest to swallow some of the cold, hard truths, and perhaps even illusions, this human experience offers. If we can return to childlike wonderment, where curiosity trumps criticism, we open ourselves to more compassion with ourselves and others. We laugh our way through this cosmic joke we call "Life". Our egos typically identify experiences as good or bad. So, having a comedic approach to living with - not for - the ego is the fastest way to "Lighten Up Enlightenment"

Egos. We all have them. In fact, egos have become a subject that more and more new thought leaders and spiritual teachers are focusing in on – inviting us to separate from, transcend above and live without. As fans of introspective spiritual work, students appreciate the works of Eckhart Tolle, Debbie Ford, Buddha, Jesus Christ and many others who have helped us observe the ego's pendulum swings between inferiority and superiority. The ego, as suggested in many works, is perceived as our "identity" – but some are finding it much easier to observe and even adjust it when they label it as an "activity". Though there are numerous ways to define and understand ego, why not add humor to such humbling practices?

Hence, the comparisons of egos to farts - a crass and comical way to observe the ego head-on from a place of neutrality and even lightheartedness. When we see our egos as more of an "activity" taking place within these "God pods" we are scooting around in, we invite in observation and inquiry versus self-judgment and criticism. Egos, much like farts, are simply another form of necessary expression in the human experience.

This new idea of "conscious" living is far more than just being mentally "here" – it is about being spiritually "present". There is a focus on being more mindful of how we show up and express ourselves in each fleeting moment. We are becoming more cognizant of how we speak to those around us, as well as, internally to self. Awareness around one's ego is the quickest way to experience enlightenment, because, as the observer of the ego, we immediately realize that we are separate from the activity taking place in our heads. Call it Soul, Spirit, Higher Self. Whatever you call it, this unexplained, undeniable essence is clearly observing the activity and identifying as distinct from the ego and its agendas.

To make this practice of mindfulness easier to "digest", here are a few brief theories that will help you identify the activity of ego within you and others, allowing you to experience enlightenment every time you practice this art of observation alone.   No different than the sometimes abrupt and offensive activity of farting, egos share a very similar M.O. :

1)   We all have them and it's easier to tolerate our own than others.
2)   We have our own unique brand - some "digest" information or experiences better than others. Some environments can be extremely offensive and upset those who are highly-sensitive to specific topics.
3)   Clearing the air can be difficult after either is "aired", typically putting a significant distance between us and our loved ones/ friends/fellow beings.
4)   Both are known to cause a set of rosy cheeks - only with ego they are topside. Expressing either can cause embarrassment - for both parties.

5) They both share the Silent But Deadly expression! C'mon, we all know that stinkin' thinkin' internal dialogue we have that we are "better than another" or "not good enough". Both can be toxic and held back when not able to express them in a safe space.

6) Often, those who express either are quick to blame, not to claim. All too often we point out and laugh at others for their abrupt explosions of fury or flatulence, but rarely do we acknowledge openly and humbly in the times that we have done the same, "It was me".

7) Pfffttt.... Just hot air. You know, those moments when you think there's solid proof of someone's incompetence, but really our perceptions of them are proven completely inaccurate. Sometimes, whether it's an ego or a fart, it expresses as nothing more than hot air.

8) Sharting is possible with both. Ever had one of those moments, when you swear you have self-control and you won't explode, but you just can't take it any longer and you get diarrhea... of the mouth (always a mess to clean up). This happens often when we have held back our opinions, rather than sharing them over time, then wind up expressing it all in an explosive rant.

9) Letting both go creates inner peace. As human beings we are meant to express. It is human nature. Both activities of farting and ego chatter are necessary to fully experience this think we call "life".

The invitation here is to consider filtering before we fire. This act of observing the ego and allowing discernment before discharge is deemed 'Conscious Cropdusting' and may just be the answer to world peace.

Here's to expressing ourselves through many unique forms in a loving and less-offensive way, creating an environment that is less-toxic and more tolerable for all humankind. Laughing our way through the everyday human foibles we share and shed."

StevieAnne Petitt is a Conscious Comedian, Author and Speaker. Her book, 'Egos Are Like Farts…' (as endorsed by a #1 NY Times Best Selling Hay House Author, Pam Grout) is offered FREE for download at her website http://stevieanne.com. She also is available and honored to serve via interactive workshops, book signings, and conscious comedy opportunities."

- StevieAnne Petitt

Art and Sacrifice; an unlikely couple

Art is a form of universal communication that speaks directly to the soul. Sacrifice is the final act in a long journey whose main purpose is to harness the soul. While the act of sacrifice is seldom beautiful or painless, its completion must be done artfully if one is to live through it and shine on towards the great human intermission.

Choices

The selfless seldom realize the difficulty of their sacrificial endeavours until it is too late for them to stop or leave or turn back. All journeys undertaken with the purest intention of heart always come to a point, or many points, where the illusory foundations of life are removed from beneath the feet; giving the impression that all is lost and life is dark and miserable.

Lost along the steep journey; on a mountainside, in the haze of fog, lying in mud, in pain and in tears, one must muster the strength to carry on. One must find their faith and hold steady to it, trusting that All is Good. To pass the great test of sacrifice, one must find the art; the honour in suffering and the beauty in contrast. If one is successful in attaining this sight when all that is temporal is aiming to blind, they will summit to a place of joy unseen by most but revered through out human history.

All journeys are different yet each and every one of us is walking along the same road. Some are farther in front and others further behind, some are jogging while some are laying down to nap, yet nonetheless we are all on the same path. We each encounter similar challenges and learn, or fail to learn, the same lessons. And though many would love to believe that we are each different when it comes to what we must learn on our evolutionary paths, we are not. Only our perceptions are different. The way we individually view the world is different. The stories and the people we fill those stories with are different. Our lessons are the same. How we choose to learn them is where individuality exists.

Choices are the fruit of life and free will is the law of this planet. Sometimes we think there is no choice and thus we do not act. Other times there are so many choices it seems impossible to choose only one and thus we do not act. Then there are times we are so focused with ambitious acuity that we block out all choices that do not serve a desired outcome. And finally there are choices in life which take you to places you never imagined; zigzag you; bring you off but then back onto your path and wake you up to a reality that is beautiful beyond belief. But in order to reach this place, one must sacrifice much.

All good stories have a beginning, a middle and an end. The beginning feels like a grand adventure as things seem new and exciting. You have energy, hope, and no concept of time. In the middle, it feels like there is no end in sight. Your hope wanes, your energy lowers with each self-made expectation that isn't met. There are ups and there are downs, highs and lows, there is misery and joy. And as you hike up, up, up the steep mountain path you must continually choose. You must choose to either wallow in the pain you feel; your sore feet and muscles, your empty stomach, your tired body. Or you can choose to find grace; the beauty that has always surrounded you and has never left your side; the warm sun hitting your skin, the clean air filling your lungs, the sweet berries you've collected along the way. Within this dualistic set of choices where one must focus on the light and not the dark, dwells the fine art of sacrifice. It is a growth in perspective. It is the forgoing of the complicated for the simple. It is the allowance of life. If you can find it, you might reach the end.

This life is a story of love, of sacrifice, of seeking, and of attainment. The people and the places are not as important, it's the insights that are worth pondering. For in this time, many will be required to sacrifice much and while each individual story will look and sound and feel different, the lessons are the same. And in the end, one's ability to sacrifice artfully will shape the future of the world as we know it.

By Jamine Aponte

Founder of inspired . wellness . lifestyle - jamineaponte.com

PART II

Community Questions

The following are questions that friends and family wished for me to answer in this book

Thank you very much for the inquiries

I hope that some of your questions are answered

In addition, I am open to the possibilities of me being incorrect

and welcome any further input and other answers

"What, in your opinion, is the importance of laughter and humor in this human experience? And perhaps an anecdote/story of a time that it helped you in your journey :)"

- StevieAnne Pettit

The cliche saying is so true, "Laughter is the best medicine."

Life can sometimes feel heavy and monotonous.

Let's uplift it with humor.

There are so many numerous times that laughter has helped me in my journey. I take my laughter medicine often.

To share it with others is an extraordinary therapy too.

Sometimes in a fit of laughter it even feels like an "Enlightenment Experience". When laughing so hard it is impossible to think of anything else. One is fully present - fully present with the ridiculous cause of the functions and fully present with the moment.

Laughter is medicine
Laughter is Zen

"Okay, so my question is this...

As I have grown and become more conscious and awake about life, I find it hard at times to relate to some of the people who I was once close to. What advice do you have around staying true to my new beliefs and also being able to spend time with the people in my life without feeling uncomfortable with our differences?"

- Megan Bennett-Welch

"Starting a personal development quest can sometimes lead to feelings of separation and distance in existing relationships.

When we are children we have similar beliefs and views as our family because we grow up around them. We choose our friends based off of similarities and how we feel when we are around them. As we get older we develop our own system of learning which causes differences within our own family and friends. This is great because we encourage each other to grow, however, it may also cause arguments or strife that haven't been present in the past.

The question is in understanding how we can still coexist in a positive manner with the people in our life when the rift between us becomes too great. What I have come up with so far is to reevaluate the relationship to see where we fit in each others' lives. It may be that we just need an adjustment in the way we converse or the activities we choose to do together. Even acknowledging the situation together can be helpful.

If the relationship appears more detrimental than healthy, it might be time to appreciate it for what it was and let them go. This can sound really harsh but if it causes negativity or brings you down any time you spend time with them then wouldn't it be worth it to all people involved to let go, maybe even for a short time, in order to create space in your lives for others more aligned with your path at the current time?"

- Megan Bennett-Welch

Thank you for your insights, Megan, and thank you for asking me to write more about it too.

Essentially, we are all exactly the same.

We each look a little different, feel a little different and have different stories to tell - but underneath it all we are exactly the same.

Keeping this in mind can make it easy to relate to anyone anywhere in the world.

You can still be a loving family member or friend with someone even if they don't agree with your beliefs and you don't agree with theirs.

Everyone just wants to be loved, treated well, fed well, feel comfortable and feel happy.

Talk about what you both have in common instead of what you disagree about.

Do fun activities that you both love to do.
Enjoy spending time not even talking at all
and just enjoying each others' presence.

Connect with that essence that you each share.
The humanity that you each share.
The simplicity that you each share.

If disagreements arise and arguments begin -
try to move on with grace.

Keep up the unconditional love
as the unifying force
above all else
Always

"Paul... I would like if you could expound on the topic of addictive behaviors and give some insights on how to approach behavioral changes."

- Margaret Stolzman

So many of us have dealt with personal addictions at some point in our lives. If we haven't then certainly we know others who have struggled.

There are numerous things that we can become addicted to from drugs, alcohol and other harmful substances to food, thoughts, emotions, spiritual materialism, addicted to other people and other possibilities.

These addictions are habits - repetitive patterns - that seem to have momentum and seem to have control over us.

Addictions are not afflictions.

We are not overcome by an addiction from an outside source.

Addictions are patterns that are repetitive from within.

Therefore, if we bring awareness to the patterns and to the root-causes that are perpetuating the patterns

then we can have insight into how to alter, slow down or
completely release the addiction.

It is always possible to create behavioral changes.

It is always possible to make progress.

It is always possible to heal from addictions -
short-term,
long-term
and forever.

It is always possible to have
complete forgiveness for oneself
and for others.

It is always possible to move on
with gratitude, purity and love.

It is always possible to be bright and clear
Moment by moment.

_____

"Firstly, please tell me what Ayurveda is, why it appealed to you, and your journey so far with it."

- Questions from Jwaydan Moyine

Ayurveda is comprehensive knowledge.

It is the science and philosophy of how to achieve health and happiness.

Ayurveda was developed in the Indian, Nepalese and Himalayan region of the world more than 5,000 years ago.

Even though it is has ancient roots it has been evolving with humanity and is completely modern and practical to this day.

Ayur translates as "Life" and *Veda* translates as "Knowledge".

Living with wisdom allows us to make the proper choices that lead to a better life in every single way.

Ayurveda appealed to me because it is so simple and effective.

Implementing the practical techniques that Ayurveda shares is a practice. Eventually, it becomes second-nature to live an Ayurvedic lifestyle full of vitality, joy and success.

My journey so far with Ayurveda is a continually progressive one.

Every day is another opportunity for evolution, learning, experimenting and enjoying.

"Secondly, why is it important that we begin to search elsewhere for remedies when we suffer bad health with minor or major illnesses and move away from the Western approach?"

There are many people who suffer from minor or major illnesses.

Oftentimes pharmaceutical drugs, allopathic medicine, surgeries and "Western" remedies are necessary. However, there are other times when conventional treatments only make things worse.

Sometimes a patient who takes a medicine for a disease experiences side-effects that are even worse than the original condition. In the end - the patient needs to recover from the original ailment - then again from the treatment.

Ayurvedic remedies using specific foods, herbs and therapies are much more gentle. Natural remedies may be more gentle - but are extremely effective - and are more sustainable with minimal to zero side-effects.

In addition, pharmaceutical drugs generally only treat the symptoms and not the root causes of ailments. When only the surface is addressed then the fundamental cause of the problem is still present and the disease is likely to return.

When to root cause of ailments is addressed then there is sustainable transformation and healing.

In Ayurveda - along with other alternative medicines - the focus is not so much about "removing problems" but more about "amplifying energy". When the Innate Intelligence and Vitality of the human body is strengthened then there is more of an ability to heal itself from within. When one's "energy" is increased then all of the automatic healing functions of the body are increased.

Herbs, fruits, vegetables and various foods contain concentrated amounts of vitamins, minerals, electrolytes, enzymes and Natural Energy. When you consume them then you are providing therapy for your body; you provide fuel for your immune system, for your cell-repair systems and for every system of your physiology.

In addition to taking natural medicines and natural foods for healing it is also important to make natural lifestyle changes.

Again, if we are to go to the "root" of a disease, we have to look at the daily habits that may be causing disturbance in the body.

Everybody knows that having bad posture can cause aches and pains; having chronic bad posture over months and years can cause more serious issues. Furthermore, there are many other kinds of habitual routines that cause disturbance in your body and your Life Force. Mental patterns and spiritual negativity are a part of this as well. Bringing awareness to these and correcting them can lead to healing in your life.

"Are there any people you've introduced this system to who have had health difficulties? Did they see dramatic changes once adapting to a lifestyle that included practices such as Ayurveda and yoga?"

I have introduced Ayurveda to the lives of many who have had health difficulties. I've provided individual consultations and coaching for 1-on-1 help. I've also provided group workshops, conferences, cooking classes and other events.

It is always wonderful for me to see how fascinated everyone is when they learn about Ayurveda.

Many times have I seen people experience their moments of realizations, their moments of healing, their moments of peace.

How fulfilling this is to witness
and to provide support along the way.

Since Ayurveda is a comprehensive treatment and holistic lifestyle change it is continually adaptable for each individual.

There is no destination - it is lifelong journey.

It may seem complex but it is simple.

It is a life full of
awareness,
positivity,
energy,
joy
and prosperity.

The Ayurvedic life is
a life that is full of
natural happiness.

PART III

Increase your Strength, Health, Wealth and Love

"Every morning we are born again.
What we do today is what matters most."
- Buddha

This is a comprehensive type of wellness
that goes far beyond just physical health

This comprehensive wellness involves
the strength
health,
wealth
and love

of your
body,
mind
and soul

Have these qualities in abundance
in all areas of your life

It is a continual journey
a continual practice
a continual growth
a continual evolution
day by day
moment by moment
Always getting better

It takes commitment
discipline
courage

It takes softness
forgiveness
ease

Strive to achieve greatness
and have contentment as well

Balance

Life has been dynamic

It's been a ride of ups and downs for me -
and maybe it has been for you as well

I've made mistakes
and I'm so sorry for all of them

After learning from it all
Now I do my best
to see the Light
to be the Light
to share the Light

This is why I am writing this part of the book:

To share some of the simple ideas and techniques that
are positive, effective and enLIGHTENing for me
and hopefully for you as well

"In a gentle way you can shake the world."
- Mahatma Gandhi

"Do not believe in anything simply because you have heard it. Do not believe in anything simply because it is spoken and rumored by many. Do not believe in anything simply because it is found written in your religious books. Do not believe in anything merely on the authority of your teachers and elders. Do not believe in traditions because they have been handed down for many generations. But after observation and analysis, when you find that anything agrees with reason and is conducive to the good and benefit of one and all, then accept it and live up to it."
- Buddha

STRENGTH

Strength of Body

"To keep the body in good health is a duty…
otherwise we shall not be able to keep our mind strong and clear."
- Buddha

Train your muscles to be
Tough
Capable
Durable

Work out hard

Lift weights
Lift your body-weight
Often

Walk
Run
Hike

Bike
Often

Practice good posture

Stand tall
Stand proud
Stand with integrity

Sit with dignity
Sit with poise
Sit like royalty

Practice constant mindfulness
of posture

Have the physical presence of being
"in the moment"

Have the presence of confidence

Be
Anchored

Kindle your metabolic fire

Feed your belly with "high-octane" fuel

Strengthen your abdominal muscles

Strengthen digestion

Keep your immune system robust

Strong exercise empowers your strong immunity

Have tenacity, will-power and determination

Be upbeat and full of energy

Invigorate your vitality

Resting well is necessary
for allowing your muscles to
rebuild,
restore
strengthen

Work out hard
rest hard

Powerful workouts break down muscle;
resting rebuilds muscle

Allow yourself to take naps

Allow yourself high-quality sleep at night
to have a high-quality training the next day

This down-time is crucially important

_____

Keep consistency
with your activities

Push your limits

Strength of Mind

"You have power over your mind - not outside events.
Realize this, and you will find strength."
- Marcus Aurelius, Meditations

"It is a strong mind that hews its way
through a thousand difficulties."
- Swami Vivekananda

"Courage is the most important of all the virtues because without
courage, you can't practice any other virtue consistently."
- Maya Angelou

Practice focus

Have clear direction of attention

Make your memory powerful

Exercise your brain just like you exercise your muscles

Do memory-boosting puzzles
and critical thinking workouts

Live a life with joyful experiences
that are unforgettable

Learn fast and learn strong
Be efficient with your study

Exercise your brain by reading your books
and writing your books

Learn from the experiences of others
Learn from your own experiences
Continue with more wisdom

Develop the muscles of virtues.
Strengthen:
your compassion
your patience
your integrity
your equanimity

Rest hard
so you can focus hard

Sleep well
Allow the brain to rejuvenate
Awaken with the mind refreshed and ready

Have the strength of mind
to be
steadfast in your virtues

If your mind ever feels anxious
depressed
uneasy
heavy
lift it up,
cheer it up
with strong exercise,
being outdoors in the beauty of nature,
being together with good friends and family
and doing what works for you.

Strength of Spirit

"Looking behind I am filled with gratitude. Looking forward I am filled with vision. Looking upwards I am filled with strength."
- Quero Apache Prayer

"Strength does not come from physical capacity.
It comes from an indomitable will."
- Mahatma Gandhi

Be disciplined

Be devoted to your higher power

Be strong in your faith

Be of service to others
to humans
to animals
to nature
to everything

Give of yourself
with dedication

Feel fervor with your faith

Be stout in your spirituality

Have the courage to question everything

Have the courage to receive the answers

Bravely experiment with your spirituality

Adventure to find the truth

Surrender...
Sometimes it takes the most strength
to surrender

Be of duty to the Divine

HEALTH

"Health is a large word. It embraces not the body only, but the mind and spirit as well;... and not today's pain or pleasure alone, but the whole being and outlook of a man."
- James H. West

"So many people spend their health gaining wealth, and then have to spend their wealth to regain their health"
- AJ Reb Materi

Health of Body

"Every time you eat or drink you are either feeding disease or fighting it."
- Heather Morgan, MS, NLC

Physical food is the physical fuel for our physical form

Fill up with "high-octane" fuel

Diversify your vitamins and minerals

Have variety in your foods and drinks

The saying
"You are what you eat"
is actually true

Be mindful of this

When you make mistakes
and eat what you know you shouldn't:
Be forgiving of yourself

Sometimes the stressful guilt we put on ourselves
is more harmful than the unhealthy food we ate

Be content with
imperfections and indulgences

No need to add extra stress

Along with vitamins and minerals
the food we eat provides:
Energy
Prana
Qi
Vitality

With this in mind
eat not just for the fullness of your belly
but also the intake of energy

"Agni" is the Ayurvedic name
for the metabolic fire
in your belly

Like a bonfire
keep it burning strong

Exercising regulates
your digestion

Keep your exercise and digestion
consistent and efficient

———————————————

Twisting movements and twisting yoga poses work particularly
well by "squeezing", "stimulating" and "flushing"
the belly's digestive organs
and kindling your metabolic fire

———————————————

Complete health is to have both "Yin" and "Yang"

One half of health is having "Yin": flexibility, suppleness,
relaxation and receiving energy

The other half of health is having "Yang": fitness, tone,
activity and exerting energy

Balance is best

———————————————

Health requires rest

Recovery

Allow your body to prepare
for future activity

Sleep
Meditate
Hibernate
Rejuvenate

Health of Mind

*"A man is but the product of his thoughts.
What he thinks, he becomes."*
- Mahatma Gandhi

"With our thoughts we make the world."
- Buddha

Feed your mind with intelligence

Our external environment provides sensory nutrition

Ingest wholesome experiences with your senses

Surround yourself with nutrition

Taste, touch, hear, feel, see
Positivity

With a clean and organized environment
your mind will feel more
clean and organized

Sometimes the mind likes to waste time;
be efficient with your thought processes

Be focused

Develop your concentration

Concentrate on your breath

Concentrate on your every movement
Concentrate on your every feeling
Concentrate on the reason why you are doing
what you are doing

Concentrate on your goal
Concentrate on success

Decide to be optimistic

Decide to see the
positivity
light
and lesson
in every situation

Decide to be grateful
and you will be surrounded by goodness always

Sleep
Nap
Meditate

Let the mind relax
Let the brain refresh

The mind that is well-rested is one with
lucidity, clarity and focused success

Health of Spirit

"Only healthy spirit
is a guarantee of health."
- Avicenna

Your body and brain need nutrition;
so does your spirit

The soul is nourished by clean natural environments

Being outdoors with
the earth, the plants, the air, the wildlife -
they all provide nutrition

The elements of earth, water, fire, air and ether -
they reflect
the elements within us

When we are outdoors with the natural elements
we feel at home

When we are "connected" to nature
we are naturally healthy

The body and brain are strengthened with exercise -
so is our soul

Build your spiritual muscles

Workout with your prayer and religious practices

Walk barefoot outside

Connect with the entire Earth

Plug-in

Connect with the Cosmos

Study space

Look up

Look at pictures

Study the universe
to study Yourself

Realize that you are a
microcosm in a macrocosm

You are within the universe
and
the whole universe is within you

We have greater health when we are
fully aware of our realty

Being knowledgable
of the universe
is healthful knowledge

Study zodiac astrology

Some things may be true,
some things may not be true;
either way you may discover insights about your life
helping you to have more awareness
and make wiser decisions

We spend so much time looking down
at our computers, phones and ourselves;
let's also remember to spend time
looking up at the sky

WEALTH

"The greatest wealth is health."
- Virgil

"It is health that is the real wealth
and not pieces of gold and silver."
- Mahatma Gandhi

"Seek not greater wealth,
but simpler pleasure;
not higher fortune,
but deeper felicity."
- Mahatma Gandhi

Wealth of Body

"Take care of your body.
It's the only place you have to live."
- Jim Rohn

Health is the greatest wealth

Be rich with strength

Be rich with vitality

Be rich with energy

Have an abundance of abilities

Wealth of Mind

"Live as if you were to die tomorrow.
Learn as if you were to live forever."
- Mahatma Gandhi

Fill your mind with priceless treasures

Be rich with memories

Be rich with wisdom

Be rich with so much to teach

Be rich with optimism

An optimistic mind
is pure opulence

_____

Offer your knowledge charitably

"The more you give
The more you receive
And then the more you receive
The more you have to give again."

Be philanthropic in sharing your
healthy philosophy

Wealth of Spirit

*"The best way to find yourself
is to lose yourself
in the service of others."
- Mahatma Gandhi*

*"Set your heart on doing good.
Do it over and over again,
and you will be filled with joy."
- Buddha*

*"It is like a lighted torch whose flame can be distributed to ever so
many other torches which people may bring along; and therewith*

they will cook food and dispel darkness, while the original torch
itself remains burning ever the same.
It is even so with the bliss of the Way."
- Buddha

Be rich with friendships

Be rich with familial love

Be rich with blissful experiences

Be rich with spiritual knowledge

Be rich with Love

Increase your spiritual wealth
with your spiritual practices

The more you invest
the more of a return you will receive

Be charitable
with your money
your time
your effort

Create good karma
for yourself
and others

LOVE

*"In doing something, do it with love
or never do it at all."
- Mahatma Gandhi*

Love with Body

Move your body;
where there is movement there is life

Love your body;
*"Where there is love there is life."
- Mahatma Gandhi*

Love every cell of your body
Love with every cell of your body

Use your muscles
your strength
your endurance
to provide love
Everywhere
to everyone

Use your legs
to walk
run
hike
bike
to bring more of your love
around your neighborhood
and around the world

Love with Mind

"The day the power of love overrules the love of power,
the world will know peace."
- Mahatma Gandhi

Fill your mind with loving thoughts

At every moment
think of love
and act with love

Soften your intellect
Soften your rational mind

Soften to the simplicity
of love

Love with Spirit

*"Being deeply loved by someone gives you strength, while loving
someone deeply gives you courage."*
- Lao Tzu

*"Love is the strongest force the world possesses
and yet it is the humblest imaginable."*
- Mahatma Gandhi

*"Hatred does not cease by hatred, but only by love;
this is the eternal rule."*

- Buddha

Love others
Everyone
with your body
with your mind
with you heart
and with your whole soul

Ask yourself the questions:
"How could I love even deeper?"
"How could I love even more completely?"

Underneath all of your stories
the essence of yourself
is pure love

Have a presence full of your love-essence

Be your love-essence
and help others to see theirs as well

Conclusion

Thank you for reading this book

Thank you for joining with us on this adventure

Thank you for being exactly who you are

Work hard for bettering yourself and your life
and at the same time
have contentment
and gratitude
for where you've been
where you're at
and where you're going

Be
Consistent
Diligent
Patient
Peaceful

You are already always amazing.

About the Author

With intensive academic studies, holistic technical trainings and
dynamic life experiences throughout the world,
Paul has been on a quest to learn and help as much as he can.

He has studied at numerous schools worldwide including the
Southwest Institute of Healing Arts in Arizona, USA.

He is trained, certified, licensed and practicing as an advanced
Yoga Teacher, Massage Therapist, Myotherapist, Reiki Master/
Teacher, Polarity Therapy Professional, Holistic Nutrition
Specialist, Health Chef, Ayurveda Specialist, Organic Permaculture
Farmer/Educator, Hypnotherapist, Life Coach, Ordained Minister
and Doctor of Divinity.

He has experience as an international wellness speaker,
author and educator.

He also proudly works with the USA Peace Corps.

He diligently works with individuals, small groups, communities
and colleagues locally and abroad.

In his first book he is happy to share with you

some unique insights
and invites you to join as a teammate
in creating a better world

He welcomes any questions, comments or collaborations
you have in mind and wishes you all the very best!